Gay Characters in Theater, Movies, and Television:
New Roles,
New Attitudes

The Gallup's Guide to Modern Gay, Lesbian, & Transgender Lifestyle

Gay Characters in Theater, Movies, and Television: New Roles, New Attitudes

by Jaime A. Seba

Mason Crest Publishers

MASON CREST PUBLISHERS INC.
370 Reed Road
Broomall, Pennsylvania 19008
(866)MCP-BOOK (toll free)
www.masoncrest.com

First Printing
9 8 7 6 5 4 3 2 1

Library of Congress Cataloging-in-Publication Data
Seba, Jaime.
  Gay characters in theatre, movies, and television: new roles, new attitudes / by Jaime A. Seba.
      p. cm.
  Includes bibliographical references and index.
  ISBN 978-1-4222-2012-2 (hardcover)   ISBN 978-1-4222-1758-0 (series)
  ISBN 978-1-4222-2013-9 (pbk.)   ISBN 978-1-4222-1863-1 (pbk. series)
  1. Gay men in mass media. 2. Lesbians in mass media. 3. Homosexuality in motion pictures. 4. Homosexuality on television. 5. Homosexuality in literature. 6. Gays in popular culture—United States. I. Title.
  P96.H63S43 2011
  791.43'6526642—dc22
                               2010017051

Produced by Harding House Publishing Service, Inc.
www.hardinghousepages.com
Interior design by MK Bassett-Harvey.
Cover design by Torque Advertising + Design.
Printed in the USA by Bang Printing.

PICTURE CREDITS

Creative Commons: pp. 10, 15, 27, 28, 29, 31, 36,
Focus Features: pp. 21, 45
Fox Broadcasting Company: pp. 51, 52
NBC: p. 54
PR Photos: p. 43
Showtime: p. 57
U.S. Centers for Disease Control: p. 39

Contents

Introduction

We are both individuals and community members. Our differences define individuality; our commonalities create a community. Some differences, like the ability to run swiftly or to speak confidently, can make an individual stand out in a way that is viewed as beneficial by a community, while the group may frown upon others. Some of those differences may be difficult to hide (like skin color or physical disability), while others can be hidden (like religious views or sexual orientation). Moreover, what some communities or cultures deem as desirable differences, like thinness, is a negative quality in other contemporary communities. This is certainly the case with sexual orientation and gender identity, as explained in *Homosexuality Around the World*, one of the volumes in this book series.

Often, there is a tension between the individual (individual rights) and the community (common good). This is easily visible in everyday matters like the right to own land versus the common good of building roads. These cases sometimes result in community controversy and often are adjudicated by the courts.

An even more basic right than property ownership, however, is one's gender and sexuality. Does the right of gender expression trump the concerns and fears of a community or a family or a school? *Feeling Wrong in Your Own Body*, as the author of that volume suggests, means confronting, in the most personal way, the tension between individuality and community. And, while a community, family, and school have the right (and obligation) to protect its children, does the notion of property rights extend to controlling young adults' choice as to how they express themselves in terms of gender or sexuality?

Changes in how a community (or a majority of the community) thinks about an individual right or responsibility often precedes changes in the law enacted by legislatures or decided by courts. And for these changes to occur, individuals (sometimes working in small groups) often defied popular opinion, political pressure, or religious beliefs. Some of these trends are discussed in *A New Generation of Homosexuality*. Every generation (including yours!) stands on the accomplishments of our ancestors and in *Gay and Lesbian Role Models* you'll be reading about some of them.

One of the most pernicious aspects of discrimination on the basis of sexual orientation is that "homosexuality" is a stigma that can be hidden (see the volume about *Homophobia*). While some of my generation (I was your age in the early 1960s) think that life is so much easier being "queer" in the age of the Internet, Gay-Straight Alliances, and Ellen, in reality, being different in areas where difference matters is *always* difficult. Coming Out, as described in the volume of the same title, is always challenging—for both those who choose to come out and for the friends and family they trust with what was once a hidden truth. Being healthy means being honest—at least to yourself. Having supportive friends and family is most important, as explained in *Being Gay, Staying Healthy.*

Sometimes we create our own "families"—persons bound together by love and identity but not by name or bloodline. This is quite common in gay communities today as it was several generations ago. Forming families or small communities based on rejection by the larger community can also be a double-edged sword. While these can be positive, they may also turn into prisons of conformity. Does being lesbian, for example, mean everyone has short hair, hates men, and drives (or rides on) a motorcycle? *What Does It Mean to Be Gay, Lesbian, Bisexual, or Transgender?* "smashes" these and other stereotypes.

Another common misconception is that "all gay people are alike"—a classic example of a stereotypical statement. We may be drawn together because of a common prejudice or oppression, but we should not forfeit our individuality for the sake of the safety of a common identity, which is one of the challenges shown in *Gay People of Color: Facing Prejudices, Forging Identities*.

Coming out to who *you* are is just as important as having a group or "family" within which to safely come out. Becoming knowledgeable about these issues (through the books in this series and the other resources to which they will lead), feeling good about yourself, behaving safely, actively listening to others *and* to your inner spirit—all this will allow you to fulfill your promise and potential.

James T. Sears, PhD
Consultant

chapter 1

The Influence of Entertainment

Every day, millions of people tune in to television shows, flock to movie theaters, and watch the lights dim on stage productions. Among them are thousands of gay and lesbian people of all races, colors, creeds, and ages. And while they may be interested in the many hot-button gay rights issues regularly making headlines across the country and sparking public debate, most are just looking for the same thing as their heterosexual peers—entertainment.

"I don't think that every story featuring a gay person has to be strenuously making (a political) point," said actor Colin Firth, who played a gay character in the 2009 film *A Single Man*, earning an Academy Award nomination. "I think we do have to see people, even if they are from a section of society which is **marginalized,**

What's That Mean?

Someone who is *marginalized* has been pushed to the outskirts of society, into a position of powerlessness.

we have to see them placed at the center of a story in a way where that can be secondary. It's just about being a human being."

In 1889, Irish poet Oscar Wilde wrote that life imitates art far more than art imitates life. In a contemporary context, this means that the fashion trends and catch phrases introduced by the latest top-rated television show or Hollywood blockbuster quickly find their way into popular culture. So when gay rights issues are depicted on the big screen or gay charac-

Poet Oscar Wilde had a flamboyant personality. His sexual orientation caused controversy in the nineteenth century, and even led to his being imprisoned for the "crime" of homosexuality.

ters are fluidly worked into the drama of a primetime TV show, popular opinion isn't far behind. The more gay characters are shown as being the regular human beings they are, the more other regular human beings see them that way. And this

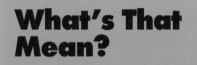

not only benefits the gay community at large, but it also impacts gay people on an individual level.

"I've known people who didn't like gay people until they saw a certain movie or a television show," said Jim Mansell. "It's kind of funny, but that's how it is. And I understand it. Seeing gay characters made me feel more comfortable with myself and who I am."

Mansell came out shortly after graduating high school in 2000, at a time when gay characters were beginning to appear on television more frequently than ever before. But that point in entertainment history was decades in the making. The gradual inclusion of gay characters and themes mirrored the increasing national awareness of gay issues in the United States.

On May 25, 1969, *Midnight Cowboy* opened in U.S. theaters. The plot revolved around a male prostitute who had male customers. The subject matter was so *controversial* that it was given an X rating from the Motion Picture Association of America, a

EXTRA INFO

Oscar Wilde was an actor, poet, novelist—and the most notorious homosexual of the Victorian era. His openness about his lifestyle, and the legal trials he faced as a result, exposed conservative nineteenth century British society to the reality of homosexuality. Despite the negative repercussion in his own life, the turmoil Wilde created helped to fuel a later movement towards tolerance of which Wilde could only have dreamed. As a young man, Wilde earned a scholarship to Trinity College and then another at Magdelen College, Oxford. He went on to win the Newdigate Prize for English verse in 1878 for his poem "Ravenna." While at Oxford, Wilde became well known for his less-than-masculine gestures and poses. In 1879, when he began to write professionally in London, his outrageous dress drew much attention. In a velvet coat edged with braid, knee breeches, black silk stockings, a soft loose shirt with a wide turn-down collar, and a large flowing tie he repeatedly offended the conservative middle class around him. He also carried a jewel-topped cane and lavender-colored gloves, and was well known for wearing in his buttonhole a flower dyed green. He married Constance Lloyd in 1884 and had two sons before admitting his homosexuality, even to himself.

Once Wilde came out, he did so loudly and publicly. As a result, he was taken to trial for his homosexuality three separate times. (At the time, homosexuality was a crime in Britain.) The first court case against him began within a week of the opening of his play, *The Importance of Being Earnest*, in 1895.

During one of Wilde's court case, he gave this emotional defense:

"The Love that dare not speak its name" in this country is such a great affection of an elder for a younger man as there was between David and Jonathan, such as Plato made the very basis of his philosophy, and such as you find in the sonnets of Michelangelo and Shakespeare. It is that deep, spiritual affection that is as pure as it is perfect . . . It is in this century misunderstood, so much misunderstood that it may be described as "the Love that dare not speak its name," and on account of it I am placed where I am now. It is beautiful, it is fine, it is the noblest form of affection. There is nothing unnatural about it, and it repeatedly exists between an elder and a younger man, when the elder has intellect, and the younger man has all the joy, hope and glamour of life before him. That it should be so, the world does not understand. The world mocks at it and sometimes puts one in the pillory for it.

Despite his eloquence, the jury was hung and Wilde was not convicted of a crime.

The next time he came to court, he again denied his proclivities but the confessions of many of his partners assured his conviction. Wilde was sentenced to two years hard labor. The judge declared, "People who can do these things must be dead to all sense of shame. . . . It is the worst case I have ever tried. . . . I shall, under such circumstances, be expected to pass the severest sentence that the law allows. In my judgment it is totally inadequate for such a case as this. The sentence of the Court is that . . . you be imprisoned and kept to hard labor for two years."

By this time, Wilde's marriage had fallen apart, his sons were taken from him, he was declared bankrupt, his house and belongings were auctioned off, and many of his friends deserted him. Within months, his play had closed, and he had been publicly humiliated.

When Wilde was released from prison, he moved to Paris with a male partner. He died when he was only forty-four.

label most commonly associated with pornography. The film also won the Academy Award for Best Picture. Less than a month after the film's release, similarly controversial members of the gay community were subjected to a police raid at the Stonewall Inn, a gay bar in New York City. The ensuing riots protesting police treatment of gay people marked a *pivotal* moment in the gay rights movement.

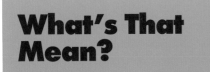

What's That Mean?

A *pivotal* event is one which is of central importance and which acts as a turning point.

This led to a growing acceptance of gay figures in mainstream culture in the 1970s, including the election of openly gay politician Harvey Milk in San Francisco. The public coming out of singer Freddie Mercury and artist Andy Warhol reaffirmed the performing arts as a tolerant environment for gay people. Albert Innaurato won an off-Broadway Obie Award in 1977 for writing the play *Gemini*, which told the story of Francis Geminiani's struggle with his attraction to another man while celebrating his birthday with his blue-collar family and neighbors. The following year, as the nation was recovering from the divisive Vietnam War, *Fifth of July* brought to the stage the story of a gay disabled veteran and his partner dealing with complicated family issues.

EXTRA INFO

Freddie Mercury, the lead vocalist of the rock band Queen, was born Farrokh Bulsara in 1946 in Zanzibar. He was known for his powerful vocals and flamboyant performances—and for his publicly gay lifestyle. He was also a practicing Zoroastrian, the religion into which he had been born, and his faith was an important part of his self-identity.

Mercury died of bronchopneumonia brought on by AIDS in 1991, only one day after he had publicly acknowledging he had the disease. In 2006, *Time Asia* named him as one of the most influential Asian heroes of the past sixty years, and he continues to be voted as one of the greatest singers in the history of popular music.

While the United States was struggling to withstand the AIDS epidemic in the 1980s, the backlash against the gay community was significant and severe. Many **conservatives** blamed the illness on homosexuality and labeled it a "gay" disease. Limited understanding of the cause of HIV and AIDS threw the public into a panic and resulted in a brewing attitude of **homophobia**. But the popular soap opera *Dynasty* was ahead of its time, progressively featuring one of America's first bisexual characters in a central role with Steven Carrington, whose storyline ultimately ended with him in a committed relationship with another man.

But the bulk of gay characters in film often fell into more dramatic categories. The horrific **hate crime** murder of gay Wyoming college student Matthew Shepard grabbed national headlines in October of 1998. The event brought increased awareness to the issue of homophobia in America, and awakened many people to the reality of anti-gay attitudes and intolerance. A year later, audiences and critics hailed the release of *Boys Don't Cry*. The film,

What's That Mean?

Conservatives are people who are resistant to change. They favor maintaining traditional values.

Homophobia is the fear and hatred of homosexuals.

A *hate crime* is a crime motivated by prejudice or intolerance.

EXTRA INFO

Andy Warhol was an American painter, printmaker, and filmmaker who was born in 1928 and died in 1987. He was a leading figure in the visual art movement known as pop art. After a successful career as a commercial illustrator, he became famous worldwide for his work as a painter, avant-garde filmmaker, record producer, and author. He was a public figure known for his membership in social circles that included bohemian street people, distinguished intellectuals, Hollywood celebrities, and wealthy patrons.

Warhol was a practicing Byzantine Catholic who regularly volunteered at homeless shelters in New York, particularly during the busier times of the year. He attended mass daily, and his art and life were influenced by his faith.

Throughout his career, Warhol produced erotic photography and drawings of male nudes. The first works that he submitted to a gallery when he was starting out as an artist were drawings of male nudes. They were rejected for being too openly gay. Warhol struggled to find a place to fit in. Other gay artists found him too "feminine," while the straight world was equally uncomfortable with him. Finally, Warhol decided, "I just wasn't going to care, because those were all the things that I didn't want to change anyway, that I didn't think I 'should' want to change." Some of Warhol's biographers have suggested that he came to terms with his sexual identity by becoming nearly invisible, even in his art. His frequent refusal to comment on his work, to speak about himself (confining himself in interviews to responses like "Um, no," and "Um, yes," and often allowing others to speak for him), and even the evolution of his pop style can be traced to the years when Warhol was first dismissed because of his homosexuality.

set against the rural Middle American backdrop of Nebraska, told the story of the rape and murder of a female-to-male transgender young man. In the aftermath of the Shepard tragedy, it struck a chord with audiences as well as critics, earning an Academy Award for star Hilary Swank.

EXTRA INFO

At the beginning of the 1980s, a mysterious disease began to be seen in gay men in New York and California. It was not the beginning of the disease—but it was the first time Americans were aware of it. It was so new and so mysterious that doctors didn't even have a name for it. They didn't know what caused it. They didn't know how it was passed from person to person. They assumed—mistakenly—that it was a "gay disease."

Scientists soon discovered that AIDS—acquired immune deficiency syndrome, as the mysterious disease came to be called—was not limited to homosexuals. It was passed from person to person through body fluids, which meant that any group of people who engaged in sex with numerous partners was particularly vulnerable to the virus's spread, as were drug users who shared needles and people who received contaminated blood transfusions.

But AIDS became mixed up in many people's minds with homosexuality. Some people even felt that AIDS was God's judgment on homosexuals.

The **sensationalism** of the media coverage of hate-motivated tragedies had prompted director Kimberly Peirce to present a different perspective. That was what led her to tell the story of Brandon Teena, whose real life death was the inspiration of the film. "I started looking at all the other coverage and a great deal of it was sensational," she said. "People were also focusing on the crime without giving it much emotional understanding, and I think that's really dangerous, especially with this culture of violence that we live in. In duplicating any sort of hate crime, I think you have a responsibility to figure out, moment by moment, what was motivating this violence to happen. Keep it personal. Keep it up close. Keep it dramatic."

What's That Mean?

Sensationalism is the use of word choice and style to startle and excite readers or viewers.

Discriminatory means making choices based on prejudices and intolerance.

By 2000, the focus of the gay rights movement had shifted to marriage equality, as Vermont legalized civil unions. More states soon followed with variations on laws that legally recognized gay couples. Other positive advancements in legal areas, including hate crimes legislation, same-sex adoption, an end to **discriminatory** employment policies, and the overturning of anti-gay laws, kept gay issues in the headlines. The result was a wave of growing public support and acceptance of gay people in *mainstream* culture.

This attitude led to the unprecedented success of the 2005 dramatic film *Broke-back Mountain,* which told the story of a decades-long relationship between two closeted gay cowboys. But the tragic love story also demonstrated Hollywood's slow movement to bringing gay characters into mainstream stories.

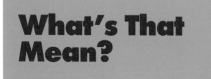

What's That Mean?

Mainstream refers to the beliefs and activities held and participated in by the majority of a culture.

"Hollywood is more comfortable with movies that show being gay as an affliction," said writer-director Alek Keshishian. "We're still at that place where it's got to be a big dramatic, political angle."

On the other hand, the television industry leapt into the new millennium by introducing gay characters into already successful shows and adding gay-themed programming to prime time slots, appealing to the coveted young audience members.

"It's been my experience that television has a much higher turnover rate in the executive arena," says Greg Berlanti, executive producer of *Brothers & Sisters*, a 2006 television series that prominently featured a gay couple. Consequently, he says, TV

HEATH LEDGER
JAKE GYLLENHAAL
ANNE HATHAWAY
MICHELLE WILLIAMS

**BROKEBACK
MOUNTAIN**

LOVE IS A FORCE OF NATURE

IN THEATRES DECEMBER 9

FOCUS
FEATURES

executives "are often much younger, and their atti-tudes about being gay can end up being much more relaxed."

Gay youth like Mansell reaped the benefits, seeing hip and relatable characters on popular mainstream television shows in various types of roles. The male half of *Will & Grace* was a successful gay lawyer who weathered the storms of being single in true sit-com style before ultimately falling in love and having a family. *Sex & the City*'s straight female characters relied heavily on the fashion sense and dating advice from their gay friends Stanford and Anthony. Demon-killing *Buffy the Vampire Slayer* saved the world with assistance from her best friend, a super-powered Wicca—but it was the witchy Willow's coming out and subsequent devoted relationship that thrust the show into the gay spotlight.

"When gay people are portrayed accurately on television and in movies, it makes us more relatable," Mansell said. "It shows people in middle America that we're normal, just like them. And it helps gay youth understand that they're not alone."

FIND OUT MORE ON THE INTERNET

Dispelling Myths of Homosexuality
www.mcgill.ca/studenthealth/information/
queerhealth/myths/

Homosexual Role Models
able2know.org/topic/121009-1

Not So Different
not-so-different.blogspot.com/2007/01/on-gay-role-models-other-day-i-posted.html

READ MORE ABOUT IT

Jennings, Kevin. *Becoming Visible: A Reader in Gay and Lesbian History for High School and College Students*. New York: Alyson, 2004.

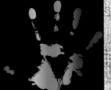

chapter 2

Out on Stage

S tage productions have historically been the birthplace of many *counter-cultural* movements in the entertainment world. The lower cost of stage production (versus either the big or little screen) frequently allows for more *progressive*, controversial issues to reach a forward-thinking audience that embraces subject matter outside the *norm*. So it makes sense that gay-themed works have been present throughout the history of American theater and that many young gay artists have gotten their first exposure in small stages and theaters. Whether in tiny art houses or under the world-famous bright lights of Broadway, gay stories presented on

What's That Mean?

A *counter-cultural* lifestyle rejects the values and behavior of the majority of society.

Progressive means favoring change and reform, rather than wanting things to stay the way they are.

The *norm* is the general, average way things are done or beliefs and values that are held.

stage have impacted the presence of gay culture in society.

"I was not an **activist**, then or now," said Mart Crowley, the gay creator of the 1968 play *The Boys in the Band*. "I didn't know what hit me. I just wrote the truth."

Before 1960, that truth was often hidden. Gay characters were not recognized, but rather implied. But even then, their influence was evident in theater around the world. In the United Kingdom, gay playwright Joe Orton achieved success with his comedic farces *Entertaining Mr. Sloane, The Ruffian in the Stair,* and *Loot*. His work earned numerous British honors, including the *Evening Standard* award for Best Play in 1966. But Orton himself was a larger-than-life character as much any of those he created for the stage, if not more. To help capture his experiences, Orton kept a diary, which he instructed should be published after his death. As a **promiscuous** and openly gay man living in London at a time when police frequently persecuted homosexuals, Orton described his adventures with various men and his run-ins with the law.

What's That Mean?

An **activist** is someone who fights actively for a cause.

Promiscuous means having casual sexual relations with a number of people.

In 1962, Orton was arrested and imprisoned for stealing and purposefully defacing seventy-two library books with his partner, Kenneth Halliwell. "Libraries might as well not exist," Orton said later to explain the incident. "They've got endless shelves for rubbish and hardly any space for good books." In response to this perceived state of literary affairs, the couple had played an elaborate prank by stealing books from the library, altering their covers and writing new blurbs on the inside flaps, and then returning them to the library.

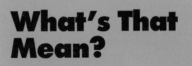

What's That Mean?

Whimsical means involving fanciful or unpredictable behavior.

An **alter-ego** is a second self, an aspect of a person's personality.

In another **whimsical** move, Orton also devised an **alter-ego** named Edna Welthorpe. Though she existed only on paper, she had significant influence on Orton's career, corresponding with his critics and even arranging to protest his own plays. As his fame increased, Orton created similar characters that increased the uproar over his more controversial work.

Like many dramatic masterpieces, Orton's short life ended in tragedy in 1967 when he was murdered at age thirty-four by his partner Halliwell, who then committed suicide. More than a decade later, *The Orton Diaries* were published, followed in 1987 by the film *Prick Up Your Ears*, which starred Gary Oldman as Orton.

In the United States, Crowley's *The Boys in the Band* became in 1968 one of the nation's first mainstream gay productions. The story revolves around a group of friends celebrating the birthday of Harold, who is dreading getting older. Each character represents a different aspect of individuals in the gay community. Michael, the host of the party, is struggling to establish his life after growing up spoiled and overindulged by his parents. As an adult, he doesn't work and instead relies on unemployment payments and other people to take care of him. He also drinks too much, and then later regrets his behavior and drinks to forget it.

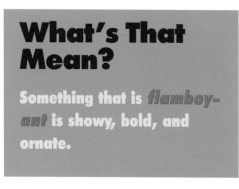

What's That Mean?

Something that is *flamboyant* is showy, bold, and ornate.

"I am still more Michael than anyone," Mart Crowley said in 2002, when he completed the play's sequel, *The Men from the Boys*. "Michael is Michael, a complex person who is aware of what is politically correct but has a sort of contempt for it."

Completing the group of guests are Larry and Hank, a couple on the rocks, the ***flamboyant*** Emory, the newcomer Donald, the lovelorn Bernard, and Alan,

Broadway in New York City has always been the site of groundbreaking cultural creativity.

an old friend of Michael's who has a secret to tell him. The story hits on some themes that eventually became common parts of other gay story lines in entertainment—Alan's apparent homophobia, a very brief past affair between Donald and Larry, Donald's desire to leave the "gay life" behind, Harold's drug use, Michael's struggle with his religious beliefs, and the memories of bittersweet romances from their youth.

Harvey Fierstein has used his talent and creativity to portray the reality of homosexual characters' lives.

Gay theater continued to progress in the 1970s, when Harvey Fierstein first staged *International Stud* in a small New York City theater. The show eventually became part of the critically acclaimed *Torch Song Trilogy*, which also included the sections *Fugue in a Nursery,* and *Widows and Children First!*

The full show debuted on Broadway in 1981, starring Fierstein as Arnold Beckoff. The story moves through the phases of Arnold's life as a Jewish drag queen living in New York City. He comes to terms with his own identity and falls in love with Alan. They decide to adopt a child, and after a tragic turn of events, the third act finds Arnold as a single father raising a gay teenaged son, David. The touching and funny tale concludes with the small family's attempts to overcome negativity and disrespect from Arnold's mother, played by Estelle Getty. The show also featured Matthew Broderick, whose performance as David won the 1982 Outer Critics Circle Award for Best Debut Performance. Fierstein won the Theater World Award in 1983.

Also in 1983, a musical adaptation of the 1973 play *La Cage Aux Folles* captured six Tony Awards, including Best Musical. The story centers on Georges and Albin, who run a nightclub in which Albin is a drag queen star. They've been together for years and are raising a son, Jean-Michel, who arrives home

la romance...
la spectacle...

LA CAGE
aux Folles
the Musical

Gary Beach   Daniel Davis
La Cage aux Folles

Music & Lyrics by   Book by
Jerry Herman   Harvey Fierstein
Based on the Play "La Cage aux Folles" by Jean Poiret

Choreographed by Jerry Mitchell

Directed by Jerry Zaks

Call 212.307.4100/800.755.4000 or visit Ticketmaster.com
N Marquis Theatre • Broadway & West 46th Street • LaCage.com

with news that he will be getting married to Anne, the daughter of a political activist intent on shutting down the local drag clubs. In an attempt to appear as a traditional family to appease the future in-laws, Albin dresses up as a woman and successfully convinces the guests he is Jean-Michel's mother. When the families go out to dinner, Albin's friend, who is unaware of the situation, asks him to sing. He does, and tears off his wig to reveal that he is really a man. Anne's family reacts badly, but when they are threatened with the press finding out about the situation, they dress as members of the club's drag performing cast before finally allowing the couple to marry.

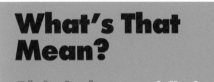

What's That Mean?

Plaintively means full of sorrow and melancholy.

As the first musical centered on a gay love affair, the show brought a new perspective on gay relationships, parenting, and drag performing. "When Mr. Hearn (playing Albin) sits in front of his dressing-room mirror to sing *plaintively* of how he applies 'a little more mascara' to make himself feel beautiful, we care much more about what the illusion of feminine glamour means to the otherwise humdrum Albin than we do about the rather routine illusion itself," Frank Rich wrote in his *New York Times* review of the show in 1983. "By making us see so clearly how precariously his self-esteem is maintained, Mr. Hearn makes it all the more

upsetting to watch what happens when that identity is attacked."

The emotional drama of being gay took another turn in the 1990s in response to the AIDS epidemic. In the first part of the decade, Tony Kushner developed the show *Angels in America: A Gay Fantasia on National Themes* in segments. The full seven-hour show debuted on Broadway in 1993 and followed the stories of couples affected by AIDS. The show was a compassionate look at the impact of the epidemic and showed AIDS patients as something other than victims. The 1996 show *Rent* also approached the topic with HIV-positive characters, including a female dancer, a straight musician, a gay professor, and a drag queen. *Angels in America* was later made into an HBO mini-series, and *Rent* was released as a full-length movie in 2008.

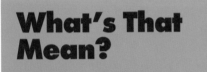

What's That Mean?

When people or things are *commemorated* they are remembered and honored.

"This disease will be the end of many of us, but not nearly all, and the dead will be *commemorated* and will struggle on with the living, and we are not going away," the character Prior Walter said in *Angels in America*. "We won't die secret deaths anymore. The world only spins forward. We will be citizens. The time has come."

FIND OUT MORE ON THE INTERNET

Joe Orton Online
www.joeorton.org

Playbill.com's Brief Encounter with Mart Crowley
www.playbill.com/celebritybuzz/article/
137446-PLAYBILLCOMS-BRIEF-ENCOUNTER-With-Mart-Crowley

SparkNotes: Angels in America
www.sparknotes.com/drama/angels/

READ MORE ABOUT IT

Sinfield, Alan. *Out on Stage: Lesbian and Gay Theater in the Twentieth Century.* New Haven, Conn.: Yale University Press, 1999.

chapter 3

Out at the Movies

In an ironic scene in the 2000 movie *The Broken Hearts Club: A Romantic Comedy*, Howie bemoans to his friends the state of gay characters in the movies. "There isn't a movie in the cinema canon that depicts a gay character that we would aspire to be," Howie complains. "What are our options? Noble, suffering AIDS victims, the friends of noble suffering AIDS victims, sex addicts, common street hustlers, and the newest addition to the lot, stylish confidantes to lovelorn women. Just once I would like to see someone who is not sick . . . and is behind on his student loans."

The Broken Hearts Club centers on Howie, played by Matt McGrath, and his circle of single friends struggling through their lovelorn lives in the gay community of West Hollywood. As players on a perpetually losing softball team, they create a family among friends, learning to accept themselves.

"A lot of people ask me when I first knew I was gay. Fact is, I don't know," says the main character Dennis, played by Timothy Oliphant. "But what I do remember, what I can recall, is when I first realized it was okay. It was when I met these guys, my friends."

Though the film never broke box office records or pulled in coveted awards, it accomplished what Howie recognized was missing from the landscape of cinema—relatable gay characters. Turned out he was on to something.

But Howie's frustrated description left out the period in cinematic history when gay and lesbian characters weren't depicted at all, at least not openly. Gay characters have appeared in American films since at least the 1930s (and arguably earlier, if one includes when Charlie Chaplin appeared dressed as a woman in *A Woman* in 1915), but they were not **explicitly** identified as being homosexual. Film experts have noted, however, that **effeminate** characters in comedies and musicals were often intended to be transparently and stereotypically gay.

Similarly, more dramatic films depicted the gay character's struggle to come to terms with his or her sexuality and sense of belonging under the guise of youthful **angst**. In the classic *Rebel Without a Cause*,

What's That Mean?

Explicitly means clearly, openly, and with detail.

When a man or boy is described as **effeminate** he has characteristics and qualities that are often considered feminine.

Angst refers to inner turmoil; a deep anxiety, often together with depression.

In the 1950s, James Dean's movie, Rebel Without a Cause, *portrayed an implicitly gay man unable to openly claim his identity—even within the context of the movie's story.*

many critics have identified the love of Plato, played by Sal Mineo, for James Dean's Jim Stark as indication that homosexuality was one of the film's many complex themes. "It is clear now but may have been less visible in 1955 that Plato is gay and has a crush on Jim," said famed movie critic Roger Ebert. "Like its hero, *Rebel Without a Cause* desperately wants to say something and doesn't know what it is."

Rebel Without a Cause was among several movies noted for gay subtext on the American Film Insti-

EXTRA INFO

For hundreds of years in England and America, homosexuality was against the law. The punishment in England ranged from being buried alive to beheading, to being burned at the stake. In America, the laws were somewhat gentler: men convicted of homosexual acts were whipped, castrated, or imprisoned.

tute's Top 100 Greatest Movies list in 2007, along with *The Maltese Falcon* (1941) and *Some Like It Hot* (1959). But much like gay people themselves, the gay characters were still in the closet.

It wasn't until the 1960s ushered in a period of social revolution that movies began to reflect the changing times. In 1961, the British film *Victim* became the first movie to use the term "homosexual" in English, six years before homosexuality was decriminalized in England. The following year, the American film

Advise and Consent starring Henry Fonda and Charles Laughton also had a gay plotline, though the term was still not used. Both films focused on a scandal, when a seemingly straight man was threatened with being exposed for a gay relationship. This began a Hollywood trend of including gay characters in tragic, controversial, or shaming situations and experiences.

Over the next few decades, gay characters began to appear in more mainstream American films. And just as Howie described, they followed a distinctive pattern.

River Phoenix played the role of the gay street hustler alongside Keanu Reeves in Gus Van Sant's acclaimed 1991 independent film, *My Own Private Idaho*.

A couple of years later, Tom Hanks earned the Best Actor Academy Award as noble suffering AIDS victim Andrew Beckett, a gay attorney fired when his employers learned of his illness, in 1993's *Philadelphia*. In the wake of the AIDS epidemic in the United States, Hanks put a human face on the illness that had defined gay life in the 1980s. What began as a story about workplace discrimination ultimately made a strong statement about the damaging effects of homophobia. And co-star Denzel Washington embodied the typical "straight guy" response. As the lawyer handling the discrimination suit, he made the journey from being repulsed at the idea of his client's personal life to accepting him as a colleague, an

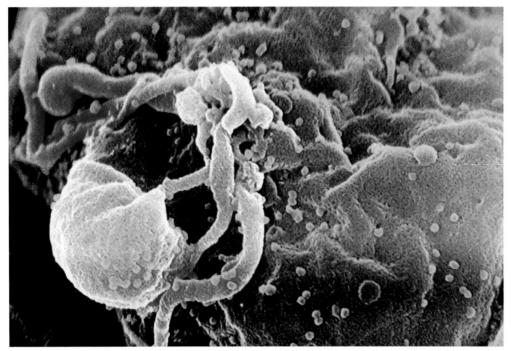

The AIDS virus—a tiny organism whose destructive power changed the world.

equal, and a friend. "By the end of the film . . . Joe has become more tolerant," Washington said of his character. "At the beginning, Joe was nervous about being in the same room with Andy; but by the end, he's actually touching him. He understands this is another human being who's hurting, and what he's labeled as shouldn't have anything to do with their relationship."

That same year, *And the Band Played On*, based on the best-selling book of the same name, chronicled the AIDS epidemic itself. As Dr. Don Francis, Matthew

Modine was the earnest young **epidemiologist** frantically racing the clock to try to trace the origin of the deadly illness for the Centers for Disease Control. The star-studded cast included Alan Alda, Ian McKellan, Glenne Headly, Lily Tomlin, B.D. Wong, Phil Collins, Steve Martin, Richard Gere, Anjelica Huston, and Swoosie Kurtz.

But not all gay characters were lost souls or tragic AIDS-stricken figures. In the case of the 1996 comedy *The Birdcage*, some were comically exaggerated **caricatures**. The film, which was based on the stage show *La Cage Aux Folles* and grossed an impressive $124 million, starred Nathan Lane and Robin Williams as a flamboyant Florida gay couple adjusting to their straight son's engagement. The twist was that his fiancée is the daughter of a conservative politician. With a wig-wearing Nathan Lane posing as a traditional happy homemaker who found a fast friend in Gene Hackman's Republican father of the bride-to-be, it stealthily brought the topics of gay parenting,

What's That Mean?

An *epidemiologist* studies the causes of diseases, how they spread, and how they can be controlled.

Caricatures are portrayals in art, film, or literature that unrealistically exaggerate certain features or characteristics.

Liberal has to do with a viewpoint that is open to change and new ideas conservative-*liberal* relations, and general tolerance into the public consciousness. It also highlighted the campy, colorful world of South Beach drag, complete with Lane's gender-bending appearance that was inspired by former First Lady Barbara Bush. "They gave me these big pearls to wear and it just became the image that everyone used," Lane said. "The sad thing is that that's what I do best—the matronly look."

The following year, openly gay actor Rupert Everett was the stylish confidante to Julia Roberts' lovelorn Julianne in the comedy *My Best Friend's Wedding*. Jennifer Aniston stepped in as the next straight girl with a gay soul mate in 1998's *The Object of my Affection*. Aniston played Nina, who fell in love with her gay best friend George (Paul Rudd). After learning she was pregnant, Nina proposed that she and George raise the child together, giving him the shot at fatherhood he'd always wanted and her the husband of her dreams. Of course, the relationship inevitably failed, but it reflected the type of gay-straight relationships that began to crop up more and more in movies. "The truth is, a friendship with a gay man can be in many ways a kind of ideal marriage," said Tony Award- and Pulitzer Prize-winning writer Wendy Wasserstein, who penned the screenplay. "If marriage is trust, the trust is there. If marriage is shared interests, often the shared interests are far more present with a gay man than with a straight one. If marriage is based on sexual attraction, many women could certainly admit that the most attractive and well-put-together men they know are gay."

Outside the mainstream, smaller scale and independent gay-themed movies began widening the scope of subject matter to lesbians and transgender characters. They also drew more big names—which led to more big audiences and critical recognition. In 1998, Angelina Jolie began her spring to stardom with a Golden Globe Award for her performance as lesbian supermodel Gia Marie Carangi in the HBO film *Gia*. The story showed the dark side of the fashion industry, as Gia struggled with the fast-paced new world. After losing her girlfriend because of her drug addiction, she soon learned she was infected with AIDS, and at age twenty-six she became one of the first high profile women in American to die of the illness. "I identified with her a lot. She's the closest character to me that I've ever played," said Jolie, who has spoken publicly about past relationships with women in her own life. "But in an odd way, playing Gia has made it possible for me not to ever become her."

Hilary Swank won her first Academy Award for the 1999 drama *Boys Don't Cry*. Set in Nebraska and based on actual events, the story follows the events leading up to the rape and murder of Brandon Teena (Swank). After moving to a new town and falling in

Ellen DeGeneres with her partner Portia de Rossi.

love with a local girl, Brandon was killed when his new friends discovered he had female genitalia.

Sharon Stone, Ellen DeGeneres, and Vanessa Redgrave starred in the 2000 HBO movie *If These Walls Could Talk 2,* which portrayed three lesbian relationships at various points in history. Beginning in 1961, Redgrave plays a retiree who is left with no property rights after the death of her partner. She is forced to leave her home, which is shown again in 1972, when it's occupied by a group of free-spirited women so enthralled by the feminist movement that they balk when one of their own dates a tie-wearing, motorcycle-driving butch lesbian. Finally, it moves to 2000, with Stone and DeGeneres as a committed couple going through the trials, and ultimate triumph, of trying to get pregnant.

Finally, in 2005, it seemed as if the gay cinematic subculture was fusing with the mainstream. Felicity Huffman starred in *Transamerica* as Bree, a biological male transitioning to a woman on a cross-country road trip with her son, who initially doesn't know her true identity. The groundbreaking work earned 2006 Oscar nominations for Huffman and Dolly Parton, who wrote the film's song "Travelin' Thru."

That was followed by the record-breaking success of *Brokeback Mountain*, which marked the first time a gay-themed dramatic film was a major critical, popular, and financial accomplishment. The film earned eight Academy Award nominations, including a win for Director Ang Lee, and took in $178 million worldwide. Often referred to as "the gay cowboy movie," the film depicts a secret romance between two married Western ranch hands. The draw of up-and-coming actors Jake Gyllenhaal and Heath Ledger led movie-goers to flock to theaters to see the first mainstream epic gay romance.

Gyllenhaal's Jack Twist met Ledger's Ennis Del Mar when the pair spent a summer tending sheep on Brokeback Mountain in Wyoming. After weeks of seclusion and bonding, the couple fell in love. And even though each went back to their "straight" lives, both marrying and establishing families, their illicit romance spanned decades. The heartbreaking story poignantly showed the isolation of their relationship and how they each struggled to cope with their situation in very different ways. When Ennis's wife Alma discovers their secret and leaves him, Jack hopes they will have the opportunity to build a life together.

Characters Jack Twist and Ennis Del Mar brought a same-sex love affair to the mainstream big screen.

But Ennis doesn't believe their relationship can exist in the open, and so it never does.

"Jack seems to be more aware and knowing. For Ennis and Alma, they have no word," Lee said. "They probably don't even know the word gay. There's no vocabulary (for them) to understand what crashed their lives, how he feels. Anything he feels in the mountain is private, even though it's wide open. At the same time, it's very private. Secrecy and privacy is the key to those characters."

But in spite of the solitude depicted in the film, the tale of desperation in love was presented in such a universal way that audiences connected with the meaning of the story, even if they wouldn't otherwise have been interested in a gay-themed film. "I was, for many years, one of those who looked away," Guy Dammann wrote in his column for the UK publication, *Guardian*. "It wasn't that I wanted to, or that there was any genuine homophobia in my attitudes. Yet I simply found I just couldn't quite cope with the sight of Rupert Everett canoodling with Michael Jenn in *Another Country*, or Daniel Day Lewis getting it on with Gordon Warnecke in *My Beautiful Laundrette*. Now, though, with the progress of cinema's slow journey out of the closet and the gentle readjustment of my sensibilities—and perhaps those of millions of others, too—I can, with pleasure."

Though some predicted that the roles would hinder or even ruin the young men's growing careers, that did not deter them from tackling the roles that ultimately earned them both Academy Award nominations. "The challenge wasn't the gay aspect of the movie," Ledger said. "In fact, in this year, 2005, I can't understand why anyone, agent, manager, publicist, would even question any actor taking any gay role." Ledger followed with high profile roles, including his Oscar-winning performance as the Joker in *The Dark Knight*. Tragically, it was a posthumous win after Ledger died in 2008.

Brokeback Mountain thrust Gyllenhaal into the limelight, and he became one of Hollywood's most sought-after young stars. He recognized the impact the film had on that turn of events. "It's been extraordinary," Jake Gyllenhaal said of the controversial role. "It has taken me to a different place in my career. Nothing but wonderful, positive things have come out of that experience."

What's That Mean?

A *biopic* is a biographical movie or television show, often including fictionalized elements.

While *Brokeback* seemed to herald the arrival of a new era in gay film, the genre was again limited to art house films and stereotyped supporting characters in mainstream movies. Then in 2008, Gus Van Sant again broke barriers to bring the *biopic* Milk to theaters. Sean Penn grabbed the Oscar for his portrayal of Harvey Milk, the first openly gay man to be elected to public office when he was voted on to the San Francisco Board of Supervisors. His colleague Dan White murdered him in 1978, and the film implied the motive was that White was actually a closeted gay man.

"The success of *Milk* has tremendous impact in creating awareness, understanding and acceptance during a time when our community continues to face opposition in our pursuit of equality," said Neil G. Giuliano, former President of the Gay and Lesbian Alliance Against Defamation. "The images of our community that these and other LGBT inclusive films bring to audiences around the country help people embrace the LGBT community with understanding and acceptance."

FIND OUT MORE ON THE INTERNET

Brokeback Mountain
www.filminfocus.com/focusfeatures/film/
brokeback_mountain

Harvey Milk Movie News
Harveymilkmovie.blogspot.com

Homosexuality in Film
www.sonypictures.com/classics/celluloid/misc/
history.html

READ MORE ABOUT IT

Davies, Steven Paul. *Out at the Movies: A History of Gay Cinema.* Manchester, U.K.: Oldcastle Books, 2008.

chapter 4

Out on the Small Screen

When audiences tuned in to the prime-time comedy *Glee* on April 13, 2009, they were treated to Kurt Hummel's lip-synching rendition of "Single Ladies." Decked out in black sequins and swaying his hips, Kurt perfected the steps of Beyonce Knowles' dance routine. The clearly gay high school student, backed up by a pair of female dancers, performed with gusto into a video camera—until his father interrupted.

"It's a unitard," Kurt said, trying to explain his attire. "Guys wear them to work out nowadays."

Viewers cringed as Kurt attempted to hide his sexuality from his father by joining the football team. And 6.6 million people were watching when the teen came out to his rough-and-tumble father, who responded with what Kurt had no doubt been waiting a long time to hear. "I've known since you were three. All you wanted for your birthday was a pair of sensible heels," said Kurt's dad. "I'm not totally in love with the idea, but if that's who you are, then there's nothing I can do about it. . . . And I love you just as much."

The Gay and Lesbian Alliance Against Defamation (GLAAD), which conducts an annual study of lesbian, gay, bisexual, and transgender (LGBT) representations in television praised the episode and the series itself. The 2009–2010 report showed that **LGBT** people accounted for 3 percent of all scripted series regular characters on broadcast television, nearly triple what it had been two years earlier. That means that out of the 600 series regular characters on five major broadcast networks, only eighteen were LGBT.

What's That Mean?

LGBT is an all-inclusive term for people who are lesbian, gay, bisexual, or transgender.

An *advocate* is someone who supports or argues for something.

"Our analysis also shows where there's still work to be done. This past year, we've seen real progress from many networks toward making their scripted programming more LGBT inclusive," GLAAD President Jarrett Barrios said of the 2009–2010 report. "At the same time, we continue to **advocate** that other networks follow suit and better reflect the diversity of the LGBT community."

Television has been home to many progressive gay characters and concepts, ever since *The Corner Bar* became the first series with a recurring gay character in 1972. The show only lasted one season, but it paved the way for more lasting characters. In 1977, comedian Billy Crystal starred in the sitcom *Soap* as the openly gay Jodie Dallas. Gay supporting and recurring characters appeared on shows such as *All in the Family, Cheers, Dynasty*, and *Roseanne* during the 1970s and 1980s.

For more than two decades, beginning in 1989, *The Simpsons* featured Homer as a traditional blue-collar father. But Homer learned a valuable lesson about tolerance in 1997 after meeting a flamboyantly gay shop owner. The rest of the family quickly

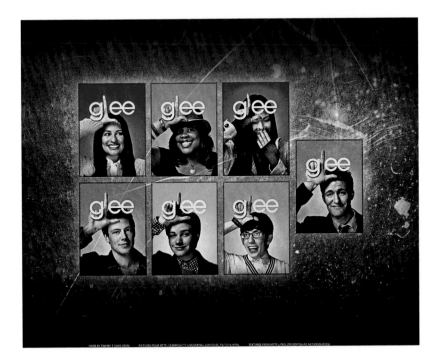

befriended John, voiced by gay director John Waters. Homer was concerned about the influence this would have on his son, Bart. After spending most of the episode, called "Homer's Phobia," trying to make sure Bart wouldn't become gay, Homer came to accept the possibility of Bart being gay after John saved his life. The show ended with him telling Bart, "Any way you choose to live your life is okay with me."

Eight years later, during a fight with his wife Marge, Homer moves to Springfield's gay district, where he bonds with his gay roommates Grady and Julio over shopping. That same year, Springfield legalized gay marriage, leading Homer to get ordained as a minister to perform the ceremonies. "And do you Julio

Even Homer Simpson stepped up to the plate on behalf of gay awareness.

take Thad to be your lawfully wedded life partner, in Massachusetts and Vermont, maybe Canada, stay out of Texas, for as long as you both are gay?" he asked one couple, referencing the segmented status of gay marriage in America. Marge's sister Patty also comes out as a lesbian, and though initially her family doesn't accept her, eventually they come around and support her.

Similar instances of familial support occurred on *Friends*, with the recurring story line of Ross and his ex-wife, Carol, who left him when she realized she was gay. Shortly after divorcing, they learned that Carol was pregnant with their son, whom she went on to raise with her new partner, Susan. When the couple planned a marriage ceremony, Carol considered calling it off because her parents refused to honor their relationship and give her away. Although he struggled with his own feelings about the wedding, Ross offered to walk his ex-wife down the aisle in a show of support. The story line continued throughout the decade-long series, which also revealed that main character Chandler's father was transgender. All of these images help send a message of acceptance and respect.

"When media images of our lives are fair, accurate, and inclusive, we find ourselves increasingly welcomed into a society that respects difference," said Joan Garry, executive director of GLAAD in 2007. "When they're not—when stereotypes and

misinformation pollute the well of cultural acceptance—we become vulnerable to anti-gay forces
working to create a world in which we do not exist."

By the time *Friends* went off the air in 2004, gay
televisions characters were a mainstay in popular
culture. *Sex and the City*'s Stanford Blatch established
the standard for the single straight girl's fashionable
gay best friend. And in 2006, *The Office* premiered
its third season by revealing that accountant Oscar
Martinez was gay. Following that episode, the series
maintained references to Oscar's life and relationships, the same as it did for the other characters.

"Sexuality of gay characters is not so central now,"
said Stephen Tropiano, author of *The Prime Time
Closet*. "Being gay is not a big deal. In some ways it
is more like the world is."

Still gay-centric television proved to be a success
when *Will & Grace* premiered in 1998
to rave reviews and ratings;
it was the most success-
ful show on television

Will & Grace *was one of
television's first popular
shows to feature a gay
character.*

EXTRA INFO

When we use stereotypes, we make assumptions about people based on the mental category in which we've placed them. According to Chinua Achebe, "The whole idea of a stereotype is to simplify. Instead of going through the problem of all this great diversity—that it's this or maybe that—you have just one large statement; it is this." We all use categories—of people, places, and things—to make sense of the world around us.

But stereotypes can also become the foundation for prejudice. "Stereotypes are categories that have gone too far," says John Bargh, Ph.D., of New York University in a recent *Psychology Today* article. "When we use stereotypes, we take in the gender, the age, the color of the skin of the person before us, and our minds respond with messages that say hostile, stupid, slow, weak. Those qualities aren't out there in the environment. They don't reflect reality."

Bargh goes on to say that stereotypes may be born out of what social psychologists call in-group/out-group dynamics. Humans, like other species, need to feel they are part of a group, and as villages, clans, and other traditional groupings have broken down, our sense of who we are has become more attached to other categories, such as black/white, straight/homosexual, male/female, fat/thin, smart/stupid, and so on. We want to feel good about the group we belong to—and one way of doing so is to look down on people who aren't in it. We tend to see members of our own group as individuals, but we view those in out-groups as all being more or less the same—as stereotypes. "Even if there is a kernel of truth in the stereotype, you're still applying a generalization about a group to an individual, which is always incorrect," says Bargh.

featuring a gay title character. The show chronicled Will, a prominent gay lawyer, and his best friend Grace, a straight interior designer. It demonstrated that a large audience for gay television shows existed, both inside and outside the gay community.

The American version of *Queer as Folk*, which originally aired in the United Kingdom, was shown on Showtime in 2000. The all-gay drama series made waves depicting a gay high school student Justin, who came out after meeting Brian, an older but less mature advertising executive. When the couple attended Justin's prom at the end of the first season, a jealous classmate attacked him. The groundbreaking show also included many similarly high-profile topics, including gay adoption, drug abuse, homophobia in politics, gay professional athletes, and workplace discrimination.

In 2004, Showtime premiered *The L Word*, a female version of *Queer as Folk* that focused on the love lives of lesbians in Los Angeles. Like its predecessor, *The L Word* also tackled hard-hitting topics including transgender issues, sexual abuse, gay marriage, gays in the military, parenting, biracial relationships, and the depiction of lesbians in Hollywood. It also included women's health issues, highlighted by the character Dana, a professional tennis player who came out on a national level shortly before being diagnosed with breast cancer. The storyline, which ended with the character's death, brought awareness to the issue of breast health for gay and bisexual women. After *The L Word* and *Queer as Folk* ended, both shows were resurrected on the LGBT-focused American cable networks here! and Logo.

Primetime network dramas also included LGBT characters, but the GLAAD study found that most of the well known examples were bisexual, including Remy "Thirteen" Hadley on *House*, Angela Montenegro on *Bones*, Ella Simms on *Melrose Place*, Alexis Meade

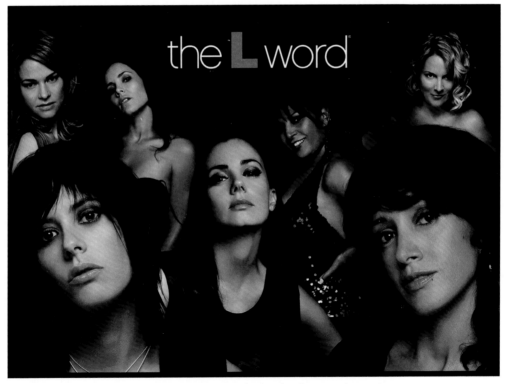

The L Word *featured dramas that appealed to both straight and gay viewers, while at the same time highlighting major gay issues.*

on *Ugly Betty*, Carmelita on *Dirty Sexy Money*, and Callie Torres on *Grey's Anatomy*.

After years of incorporating gay patients and minor storylines, *Grey's Anatomy* introduced a lesbian love story between Torres and Erica Hahn in 2008, the show's first major gay storyline. Shortly before that blossoming romance finally became a reality, the doctors at Seattle Grace Hospital treated an active soldier with a brain tumor—and a secret gay lover, a fellow serviceman. When the ill soldier's father discovered their relationship, he was separated from his partner and unable to say goodbye before the surgery that ultimately led to his death.

"It's promising to see not only an increase in the quantity of LGBT characters but that storylines about the LGBT community are becoming more reflective of current issues impacting our lives," said Barrios. "Americans now have the opportunity to see LGBT couples marrying on shows like *Brothers & Sisters*, raising children on *Modern Family*, and LGBT youth coming out on *Glee*. As more and more Americans see fair and accurate images of our community and the issues impacting our lives reflected on the small screen, they come to accept and better understand their LGBT family members and neighbors."

FIND OUT MORE ON THE INTERNET

How Homosexuals Are Portrayed on Television
socyberty.com/gay-lesbians/how-homosexuals-are-portrayed-on-television

The L Word
www.sho.com/site/lword/home.do

READ MORE ABOUT IT

Becker, Ron. *Gay TV and Straight America*. Piscataway, N.J.: Rutgers University Press, 2006.

Tropiano, Stephen. *The Prime Time Closet: A History of Gays and Lesbians on TV*. New York: Applause Books, 2002.

BIBLIOGRAPHY

Allen, Jamie. "'Boys Don't Cry' Filmmaker Saw Past Violence to Love." *CNN,* October 22, 1998.

Applebaum, Stephen. "Heath Ledger: Brokeback Mountain Interview." *BBC*, January 2006.

Ayers, Dennis. "Billy Crystal's Place in Gay Pop Culture History." *AfterElton.com*, Oct 12, 2007.

Ayers, Dennis. "Grading the Majors." *AfterElton.com*, March 25, 2007.

Cavagna, Carlo. "Interview: Ang Lee." *Aboutfilm.com*, December 2005.

Dammann, Guy. "How Gay Films Made Me a Better Man." *Guardian (UK)*, December 10, 2008.

"Denzel Washington, Tom Hanks Star in *Philadelphia* Movie about AIDS." *Jet,* January 31, 1994.

Ebert, Roger. "Rebel Without a Cause (1955)." *Chicago Sun-Times*, June 19, 2005.

Gorman, Bill. "TV Ratings Wednesday: *Modern Family, Cougar Town* Start Strong; ABC Challenges CBS." Sept. 24, 2009.

Hinckley, David. "Before 'Bruno': A Brief History of Gay Characters in Movies and TV." *Daily News*, 8 July 2009.

"Interview: The Birdcage." *Premiere Magazine*, 1996.

Lefkowitz, David. "Innaurato's *Gemini* Gets First Major NY Mounting Since Bway Smash, May 26–June 27." *Playbill,* June 16, 1999.

Miller, Samantha. "Rising Son." *People*, June 22, 1998.

Morris, Gary. "A Brief History of Queer Cinema." *GreenCine*, March 30, 2007.

Nasson, Tim. "On Top: In *Brokeback Mountain.*" *Wild About Movies*, December 9, 2005.

Orton, Joe. *The Orton Diaries.* New York: Harper & Row, 1986.

Pickard, Anna. "Glee: Season One, Episode Four." *Guardian (UK)*, 25 Jan 2010.

Rich, Frank. "Just How Gay Is the Right?" *New York Times*, May 15, 2005.

Rich, Frank. "Stage: The Musical 'Cage Aux Folles.'" *New York Times*, August 22, 1983.

Roca, Octavio. "'Boys' to 'Men.'" *San Francisco Chronicle*, 2002.

Snead, Elizabeth. "'Gia' Taps Angelina Jolie's Wild Side." *USA Today*, January 29,1998.

Stack, Tim. "'Glee' Recap: Kurt Comes Out a Winner!" *Entertainment Weekly*, Sept. 24, 2009.

Vary, Adam B. "Gay Hollywood: Out of Sight?" *Entertainment Weekly*, October 25, 2007.

Wasserstein, Wendy. "And Next Year's Oscar Goes to . . . a Deeper Kind of Love." *The Advocate*, March 31, 1998.

Weese, Brooke J. "Out of the Closet and into Primetime." *MTV/ Medill News Service*, 2007.

Wilde, Oscar. "The Decay of Lying: An Observation." *Intentions*, 1891. Memphis, Tenn.: General Books, LCC, 2010.

INDEX

ABOUT THE AUTHOR AND THE CONSULTANT

Jaime A. Seba's involvement in LGBT issues began in 2004, when she helped open the doors of the Pride Center of Western New York, which served a community of more than 100,000 people. As head of public education and outreach, she spearheaded one of the East Coast's first crystal methamphetamine awareness and harm reduction campaigns. She also wrote and developed successful grant programs through the Susan G. Komen Breast Cancer Foundation, securing funding for the region's first breast cancer prevention program designed specifically for gay, bisexual, and transgender women. Jaime studied political science at Syracuse University before switching her focus to communications with a journalism internship at the Press & Sun-Bulletin in Binghamton, New York, in 1999. She is currently a freelance writer based in Seattle.

James T. Sears specializes in research in lesbian, gay, bisexual, and transgender issues in education, curriculum studies, and queer history. His scholarship has appeared in a variety of peer-reviewed journals and he is the author or editor of twenty books and is the Editor of the *Journal of LGBT Youth*. Dr. Sears has taught curriculum, research, and LGBT-themed courses in the departments of education, sociology, women's studies, and the honors college at several universities, including: Trinity University, Indiana University, Harvard University, Penn State University, the College of Charleston, and the University of South Carolina. He has also been a Research Fellow at Center for Feminist Studies at the University of Southern California, a Fulbright Senior Research Southeast Asia Scholar on sexuality and culture, a Research Fellow at the University of Queensland, a consultant for the J. Paul Getty Center for Education and the Arts, and a Visiting Research Lecturer in Brazil. He lectures throughout the world.